SHARING GOD'S LOVE

The Jesus Creed for Children

SHARING GOD'S LOVE

The Jesus Creed for Children

Scot McKnight &
Laura McKnight Barringer

Illustrated by Dave Hill

PARACLETE PRESS
BREWSTER, MASSACHUSETTS

2014 First printing

Sharing God's Love: The Jesus Creed for Children

Text copyright © 2014 by Scot McKnight and Laura McKnight Barringer
Illustrations copyright © 2014 by Paraclete Press, Inc.

ISBN 978-1-61261-581-3

The Paraclete Press name and logo (dove on cross) are trademarks of Paraclete
Press, Inc.

Library of Congress Cataloging-in-Publication Data

McKnight, Scot.
  Sharing God's love : the Jesus creed for children / Scot McKnight and Laura
McKnight Barringer.
    pages cm
  ISBN 978-1-61261-581-3 (trade pbk.)
  1. Love—Religious aspects—Christianity—Juvenile literature. 2. God
(Christianity)—Worship and love—Juvenile literature. I. Title.
  BV4639.M385 2004
  241'.4—dc23   2014025151

10 9 8 7 6 5 4 3 2 1

Published by Paraclete Press
Brewster, Massachusetts
www.paracletepress.com

Printed in the United States of America

Aksel and his little sister Finley eat breakfast together. This morning, like every morning, Aksel and Finley say the Jesus Creed, as Jesus taught:

"The Lord our God, the Lord is one. Love the Lord your God with all your heart. Love other people as yourself."

"Bye, Aksel!" says Finley as she watches Aksel put on his puffy snowsuit and boots for the trip to school.

"Bye, Finley!" says Aksel.

"Do you want to sit with me?" Aksel asks Jaslynn on her first day at a new school.

"This is my favorite place on the bus," Aksel says.

He walks Jaslynn to the seats that have big bumps for feet to rest. Aksel remembers,

Love other people as yourself.

Back at home, Finley's mom asks her, "Finley, please put your dolls where they belong."

Finley remembers,

Love God with all your heart.

She lines up her dolls in their special small crib and counts them, "One-two-three!"

"I brought you a donation for the food drive," Aksel says to the school principal as he walks to his classroom, soup can in hand. "It's my favorite soup when my throat feels scratchy."

"Good choice, Aksel! You are feeding a hungry person." Aksel remembers,

Love other people as yourself.

✿

"Some of your clothes do not fit you any longer, Finley," her mom says. "We will give these to children who need them." Finley remembers,

Love other people as yourself,
as she helps her mom pack clothes into boxes, even her blue-and-yellow striped dress and matching shoes.

"These are my favorites!" she says.

Mrs. Shogren asks for a volunteer to help her pass out glue. Students need glue to stick wiggly eyes on owl projects. Aksel raises his hand and offers to help his teacher. Even though he drops the glue, he feels good for helping. Aksel remembers,

Love God with all your heart.

"Can Caleb come over to eat lunch with me, please?" Finley asks her mom.

"Sure," mom responds.

"THANK YOU SO MUCH!" Finley says with delight. She squeezes her mom's neck super tight, and she remembers,

Love God with all your heart.

The lunch monitor at Aksel's school looks concerned. "Boys and girls, it is very noisy in here. Please use inside voices," he says to everyone. Aksel remembers,

Love God with all your heart.

And then he chooses to use a softer voice as he tells James and Andrew about his squishy ketchup packet.

Finley and Caleb eat chicken nuggets for lunch. They nibble the nuggets so the nuggets look like bird beaks. Finley laughs and says, "That's a long bird beak!"

"Thank you," answers Caleb. Finley remembers,

Love other people as yourself.

"Let's swing together," Aksel says to Jack, who stands alone on the school playground.

"Let's try to go really high, like SUPER HEROES!"

Jack says, "This is the best day of my life!" Aksel remembers,

Love other people as yourself.

Finley wants a glittery purple purse, just like the happy girl on television.

"I really, really want that glittery purple purse!" Finley shouts to her mom.

"We're not going to buy that, honey. Let's be thankful for the purses you already have," her mom says.

Love God with all your heart,
Finley remembers. Then she decides to play with her red purse with the long handle and shiny gold zipper.

"Grace, I noticed you have blue paint on your paint brush. You can borrow mine for your yellow sun."

Grace loves how her yellow sun looks bright and shiny. "Thank you, Aksel," says Grace. Aksel remembers,

Love other people as yourself.

Finley colors a picture for her mom. "I drew a giraffe for you!" she says.

"Thank you, Finley. I like the colors you used. Purple and yellow look great on giraffes." Finley remembers,

Love other people as yourself.

"I picked dandelions for you at recess!"

"Why, thank you, Aksel," says Mrs. Shogren, placing the sticky bouquet on her desk. "I will think of you whenever I look at them."

Love other people as yourself.

Finley's mom walks her to ballet class.

"You leap like a graceful ballerina, the best I've ever seen!" Finley tells Betty, one of the girls in her class.

"Thank you!" Betty says, smiling back at Finley.

Love God with all your heart.

"You kick the ball farthest," Aksel tells Carter in gym class. "You kick it so high!"

Carter grins and looks proud. Aksel remembers,

Love other people as yourself.

Finley and her mom stop at the toy store to buy a birthday present.

"I want one, too!" Finley yells, when she sees the rainbow snow cone maker.

"Finley, it is not your birthday," her mom says. "This is a present for Ethan." Finley remembers,

Love God with all your heart.

"Okay," she says.

Aaron feels bad because he thinks he is not good at using scissors. Some kids point at his squiggly edges. Other kids giggle at his squiggly edges.

"Aaron, try your best! It is not important if your edges are squiggly," Aksel tells Aaron.

Love other people as yourself.

"Finley, it's nap time. Please lie down quietly in your bed," mom says.

Finley hugs her stuffed animal George and rubs his furry brown head. "Nap time, George. Time to be quiet," she tells George. Then she remembers,

Love God with all your heart.

During naptime at school, Mrs. Shogren reminds students to lie quietly.

"Shhhhhh," Aksel whispers to Ellyn. They both stop talking and close their eyes tightly. Aksel remembers,

Love God with all your heart.

Finley decides to surprise Aksel when he gets home from school. She hides behind the green curtains, waiting patiently for the front door to open. She plans to say, "Hi, Aksel!"

Love other people as yourself.

"See you tomorrow!" Aksel calls to Mr. Balis when the bus stops at his house. "Thanks!"

"Have a good evening, Aksel," Mr. Balis smiles.

Love other people as yourself.

It is dinnertime. Aksel and Finley sit together with their mom and dad. Mom and dad ask how they loved God and other people today.

"I picked dandelions for my teacher," says Aksel.

"I told Betty she is a good ballerina," says Finley.

Together they hold hands and say,

"The Lord our God, the Lord is one. Love the Lord your God with all your heart. Love other people as yourself."